T0194994

Rosalee, the PW

MARCY LYTLE

WESTBOW
P R E S S®
A DIVISION OF THOMAS NELSON
& ZONDERVAN

WestBow Press books may be ordered through booksellers or by contacting:

WestBow Press
A Division of Thomas Nelson & Zondervan
1663 Liberty Drive
Bloomington, IN 47403
www.westbowpress.com
1 (866) 928-1240

ISBN: 978-1-9736-3771-4 (sc)
ISBN: 978-1-9736-3770-7 (hc)
ISBN: 978-1-9736-3772-1 (e)

Library of Congress Control Number: 2018910014

Print information available on the last page.

WestBow Press rev. date: 10/17/2018

INTRODUCTION

My mom was one of a kind. Everyone who knew her was amazed by her business savvy, her kind heart, and her flair for fashion … all the way until her last breath. She was a business entrepreneur and became highly successful, she gave generously to family as well as to strangers, and she had this incredible keen eye for color and design when it came to creating clothes or outfits.

I admired and loved my mom, and I was greatly grieved when she unexpectedly passed on June 12, 2017. Part of the process of healing and working through that grief was remembering and writing down all of the funny things she said, the ways she delighted in me and others, and the hidden sadness, mixed with the joy of life, that I knew was there behind her beautiful smile.

One day, not long after she passed, I asked the question, "What are you doing, Mom?" And the answer I received became the catalyst for this story of a preacher's wife and the life she never wanted but lived to the fullest.

I hope you enjoy this book and come to know my mother for the wonderful woman she was and will always be to those of us who knew her well.

Marcy Lytle

CHAPTER 1

The Square

It was Saturday at 11:00 a.m., and Lovey said she'd meet Rosalee on the square to watch people.

That was what all of the girls did on the weekend, unless, of course, they were working at the local drugstore behind the soda fountain. That particular job was the best because every friend in the neighborhood stopped by to enjoy a milkshake and visit, which was great fun. With her hair pinned back because it was a bit windy on this October day, Rosalee actually skipped down the street. She had once read, or maybe her mom had mentioned it to her, that skipping could define a girl's calves quite well. So skipping Rosalee did!

Lovey was Rosalee's best friend, and they met up as often as they could to sit on the grassy lawn. They enjoyed watching the shoppers on the square as they showed up at the only place in town where food was served, there was stuff to buy, and people to greet.

"Hey, Lovey!" Rosalee waved as she met her friend at their favorite spot.

"Rosy!" Lovey waved back with a vigorous hand

movement that was quite recognizable; Lovey showed all of her emotions with her hands.

Lovey always looked great with her blond, wavy hair. Rosalee had recently cut her own hair into a bob, but it was straight and dark. She often envied Lovey's locks, but she knew her own hair was quite pretty when she fixed it just right. The sun shone so perfectly on Lovey's hair and made the natural blonde color come to life, almost like honey dripping from a honeycomb.

Charles and Lina Blevins, Rosalee's mom and dad, lived just off the square—two blocks, to be exact. Lina could see the courthouse from the backyard, where she carefully hung clothes out to dry. Whites went on one line and colored clothes on another. That was how she had learned to do it from her mom. Lina could easily call for Rosalee to come back home if she needed her help at the house. It was a modest house for those days—just painted white wood with black trim. Inside were an upright piano, where Lina often entertained the family at night, and a china cabinet, where Lina displayed her favorite dishes, collected over the years. Something was always cooking on the stove because Lina liked to see her kids (and visitors) eat. Charles enjoyed eating too, especially Lina's macaroni and cheese. All that creaminess was the best, according to just about everyone who tasted it. She almost overcooked the big noodles and somehow made the American cheese look irresistible as it hugged the inside and outside of each individual elbow, with all pieces swimming in butter.

Boy, was it good! That recipe would last a lifetime and beyond.

Rosalee lived at home with just her parents. Her older brother, Charles Jr. (everyone called him Charlie) was off to war, along with most of the other boys in town. The year was 1944, and one reason Rosalee enjoyed skipping away to the square so much was to get away from the sad faces of her parents, who missed Charlie so much. Oh, he wrote letters and all, but it just wasn't the same as having him swing the front door open and yell, "What's for dinner, Mom?"

Rosalee missed Charlie too, but he was six years older than her, so they never really had much in common. He was the older brother and she the younger sister, and that was that.

As Rosalee pressed out the front of her dress that had gotten crumpled and wrinkled from the walk, she was explaining to Lovey how she'd gotten this new fabric and sewn on this fashionable collar—just a little bit askew—for something a bit different. Since Rosalee could remember, she'd always liked something out of the ordinary in her style. Her dad wouldn't allow her to cut her long hair until she was thirteen, so on that very birthday, Rosalee marched to the nearby salon and had her hair shortened to above the shoulder. And when she sewed, she often thought, *Why create a masterpiece that looks like everyone else?*

Lovey exclaimed, "Rosalee, that's the best!" when she saw the collar against the smooth print, turned just a bit sideways for flair.

"Thanks, Lovey!" Rosalee replied as she felt the collar again. She'd just finished attaching it a few days prior when she had that inspiration to sew it askew.

Askew happened to be a word Rosalee learned in grade school and had never forgotten because it sounded so much like *achoo*, and that amused Rosalee.

Some of the girls met at the city pool to bask in the sun in their new swimsuits and talk about the few young men who were left in town for the picking. Picking *for a date*. Rosalee didn't swim, though. Her dad was a preacher, very conservative, and didn't think it was quite right to wear that revealing attire in public. *And to swim with boys?* That was just not going to happen as long as Rosalee lived under his roof! The city pool wasn't very far away either, but Lovey was content to meet Rosalee on the square instead of joining the other girls, so there they sat. Lovey could swim any time she pleased, but to sit with her best friend and watch people come and go—well, she wouldn't miss that for the world!

They each held ice cream in one hand, and the other hand moved in rhythm to the words from their mouths; squeals of delight emerged as they shared secrets. Rosalee and Lovey noted the shoes on this lady and the handbag carried by that girl. Watching people and chatting really was the best pastime in the world for a lazy weekend afternoon.

CHAPTER 2

Clouds and Charlie

Despite not being allowed to swim in the local pool, Rosalee did grow up around water. Her skin was tanned and dark because she played by the river behind her house when her brother was home—back when they had lived in Arkansas.

Lina often opened the back door and asked, "What are you kids doing?"

Rosalee mostly replied, "Just juning around." That meant, "Nothing, really. Just hanging out."

Charlie taught her the names of the trees next to the water. They stood and skipped stones, and they reclined in the grass and saw pictures in the clouds. Once, Charlie saw an entire fleet of ships sailing by, and Rosalee mostly saw the beautiful hues of blues and grays instead of shapes and things. But Rosalee never stepped one foot in the water. If her dad said swimming with boys was evil, then she figured something was bad about the water itself! It just looked too scary.

"Charlie, is swimming fun?" Rosalee asked her brother. He often sneaked a dip under the water when Lina and Charles were away from the house.

"It sure is! You're really missing out, sister," Charlie replied as he reached over to tickle her under the neck. Then he sauntered off back to the house to find a snack to eat. Rosalee's brother sure could eat!

CHAPTER 3

Tent Meetings

Charles Sr. was one of those preachers who rode around town in a horse-drawn buggy, and he set up tent revivals. A tent revival was just a large tent set up in a vacant grassy area, open on the sides, with a big sign stuck in the ground nearby that welcomed all sinners and those who needed to repent. Most of the signs were handmade out of an old box affixed to a wooden post. Wherever God told him to set up and preach, Charles did. He said the Holy Spirit would come, and people would know all about the power.

Was that a *ghostly* spirit? Rosalee wondered sometimes.

Her dad would open his Bible, talk about the Holy Ghost, and raise his hands as if he'd seen a real one—a spirit with shape and all!

"Repent of your sins!" he'd command with one finger pointing to each person under the tent.

The people sat on hard chairs. They were given paper fans to blow against their hot faces, and little kids cried and sweated and sometimes ran around. And almost every time a tent revival took place, several people got up at the end and made their way to the altar (a wooden bench, if there was one to be had, or maybe just a dry patch of grass). There, they knelt, and tears flowed. Men crouched down on one knee, hat off and in hand, and wept like little boys. Women wailed and raised their hands in surrender, only there were no white flags. However, a few waved handkerchiefs that looked like white flags. Whatever wrongs they'd done, their weeping, wailing, kneeling, and fanning gave way to smiles and hugs from Rosalee's dad as he prayed with each one. They had been washed clean and then were led to the river for baptizing.

Rosalee never understood why the river was the place to go for such rejoicing when she couldn't even get in it with her friends. But she didn't dare ask. She supposed baptizing was different. She supposed in that water, where the Holy Spirit hovered over the top like a dove frozen in midflight, girls and boys didn't look at each other with a wrong desire. Yes, that was probably the difference. And, of course, all of the people being dunked were fully clothed.

CHAPTER 4

Saturdays

This particular Saturday, however, there was no tent revival, so Rosalee was free to sit and watch people with Lovey. It was "good people-watching," as they called it, and they did it together until every last bite of the ice cream was licked and just about every person in town had walked past.

Rosalee pointed to that girl over there, remarking to Lovey, "Aren't those shoes the cutest?"

Lovey smiled as she replied, "Oh yes, girl!"

And they both right then and there decided to save up for a new pair of open-toed heels of their own. Rosalee and Lovey stood up and noticed a couple of other friends who had arrived on the lawn in new shoes, new dresses, and fresh styles. Rosalee wasn't sure quite why she loved fashion, but she did with all her heart. It seemed her mind was always churning up colors and buttons and zippers and sleeves, in all sorts of ways, on bodices and skirts. It's all she wanted to dream about, talk about, or look at on a Saturday afternoon. And once in a blue moon, she'd dream about swimming with the boys, but then she'd go back to buttons and zippers. She had learned that an "idle mind is the devil's workshop" from her mom, so she didn't linger too long by the pool, in her thoughts ...

Saturdays on the square were decidedly the best, the best times to be had in Rosalee's sheltered life away from water, boys, and red lipstick—which she was only allowed to wear in moderation, now that she was sixteen. The war raged on across the seas, preaching went on down the street, and Rosalee felt fabric as it slid underneath the needle of the sewing machine in the evening, when the people-watching was over. She enjoyed humming all of the popular tunes while she sewed. Singing was definitely an okay pastime to have, for a young girl whose dad was a preacher.

Rosalee didn't really let her mind wander all that much because it didn't serve her well. Questions weren't supposed to be asked. There were really no good answers; and there was so much fabric and so many ideas to be paired with those fabrics, so why not focus on that? As the sun set on Saturday evening and Rosalee knew that Sunday morning was coming, she often smiled sweetly as she hemmed up the skirt she'd just attached to the bodice of the new dress she was planning to wear for Sunday service. Church was one place where she could dress up in her finest creations all made from the pictures in her mind, after watching the ladies on the square that Saturday afternoon.

CHAPTER 5

The Letter

Rosalee's brother, Charlie, wrote home, and the letter arrived one Monday in November. He had scribbled a bit about rations and Kitchen Patrol (KP) but then told his parents about a fellow soldier named Melvin. And to the Blevins' surprise, they realized Melvin was indeed the son of Virgil and Eunice Clearman, a couple whom Charles Sr. had married at one of the churches eighteen years prior. You see, Charles Blevins was older than most dads of older teens. But Virgil Clearman was younger. So somehow it happened that these two fellow soldiers in the war had a connection of the most coincidental kind. Indeed, it was a small world.

The next day, a letter arrived for Rosalee—not from her brother Charlie but from Melvin! Rosalee sat the letter aside because she already had a date for the evening with Darrell and didn't have time to open a note from another boy. It was a Tuesday, not a normal date night, but Darrell worked at the local farm on the weekend and most weekdays, with Tuesday being his day off.

Rosalee didn't really care that much for Darrell, but she'd go anywhere with pretty much anyone for an excuse to wear her new dress—the same one with the skewed collar. She got so many compliments when she wore it!

Would Darrell notice? Rosalee wondered.

Oh well, it didn't matter. Rosalee never dressed for someone else or wore what they wore. She dressed to please herself, and pleased she was! She even wore the new open-toed sandals she'd gotten after seeing that girl on the square wearing a pair! They were a bit higher in the heel than she was used to, but that was okay. Darrell was a bit tall, so she'd fit perfectly next to him, arm under arm.

She turned and twirled in the mirror, a wood-framed, rather large mirror that was hanging in her parents' bedroom. Lina and Charles ran a used furniture store and often held onto pieces that were useful. This mirror was Rosalee's favorite! She always dreamed about that one day when she'd have her own home and bedroom, and she'd hang a mirror on the wall that would light up the room as it caught the sun's rays through the window across on the other wall. Maybe when she married, her mom would give her this mirror! *Oh, could it be so?*

Darrell showed up, and the couple walked hand in hand to the square. One soda shop was open, and music was playing as they opened the door to walk inside. It was a great song everyone loved, "Don't Sit under the Apple Tree with Anyone Else but Me." Darrell and Rosalee sipped on a Coke as they listened and others danced.

Dancing was right there with swimming: it was something one didn't do in public and never with boys. Rosalee watched and enjoyed all of the moves everyone made, but she just listened to the lyrics and sipped and smiled. Oh, she wanted to dance. She thought it looked like great fun, but she squelched that desire straight away. She didn't want her mind to become "the devil's workshop" if she let her thoughts drift too far from holy thinking. What was the devil's workshop anyway, and what was crafted there? Was it like Santa's workshop, with little green elves? Surely, the devil's elves must have horns—stubby red ones, for sure.

Rosalee turned her attention back toward her date.

Darrell did not notice Rosalee's new dress, and Rosalee didn't notice that Darrell didn't say anything. She was thinking about that letter she had laid aside back home and wondered why her brother's friend wrote her a note. What did he have to say to her? She'd have to open her drawer and read it before she went to bed. For now, it was tucked underneath her stockings, the stylish ones with the line up the back of the leg, reserved for special occasions. She had opted not to wear them tonight on her date with Darrell because they weren't really that comfortable. The waistband was tight, and she was afraid of snagging them and causing a runner (a snag that becomes a long streak), so that pair of pantyhose stayed in the drawer.

CHAPTER 6

Melvin

Later that night, about 9:30 p.m. to be exact, when the date with Darrell was over and Rosalee was back at home, she sat alone by the lamp on her desk. She had put her dress to the side to be washed, placed her new shoes in the cardboard box and back on the high shelf in the closet, and the house was quiet. All she could hear was the wind outside the window, indicating the weather was changing to colder temperatures overnight. After all, it was getting close to Christmas. Her desk was small. It was another piece from the furniture store, and the drawers squeaked when they were opened. She'd have to ask her dad to oil them for her tomorrow.

Quietly, she opened the drawer and pulled out the letter, especially careful not to wake her parents. They were sound sleepers, so all was well. Rosalee sat in a straight-back, cane-bottom chair, and she opened the Air Force stationery and began to read.

Dear Rosalee …

It wasn't a long letter, and it was mostly Melvin introducing himself and stating his rank and duties while stationed in France. *My, how exciting France must be!* thought Rosalee. He wrote how he wanted to be a pilot, but he was left-handed, so he wasn't allowed. Right at that moment, Rosalee felt sorry for Melvin.

"Why shouldn't left-handers be allowed to fly planes?" she actually whispered aloud.

She then laughed silently because Rosalee wanted to be a famous fashion designer but no way was that happening, either! Not because she was left-handed, but she didn't have the money for school. Oh, she'd often let her mind wander to what life would be like if she could be a fashion designer—all that fabric and all of those colors ...

Rosalee had never met a left-handed man. Melvin sounded interesting, so she kept reading. He talked fondly of his mother and father and four siblings back home. He was the eldest of five. This information made Rosalee smile again, as she fondly thought of her brother and missed him so much. She even chuckled once more when she remembered her brother telling her that when he was smaller, if he disobeyed, Lina placed him in a dress to sit on the front porch for all the people passing by to see! She was sure there was something gravely wrong with that sort of discipline, but the thought of her brother in a girl's frock made her laugh.

As she read further, Melvin told Rosalee that Charlie had a picture of her and had shown him. It was a photo of her posing next to a car, kicking her leg to the side, as she loved to do. Rosalee loved a good photo of herself. She wasn't prideful. She just enjoyed the camera and looking good for it. Melvin mentioned her nice dress and how Charlie had told him that Rosalee was quite the seamstress! Rosalee's heart pounded just a bit.

This man noticed my dress!

As the letter ended, Rosalee folded it carefully and tucked

it away under her stockings once again. She slowly stood up from the chair, still careful not to make a peep. She sort of slid across the hardwood floor to her bed, feeling a bit of a skip in her step. But skipping would have to wait until morning.

Rosalee went to sleep dreaming about this kind young man who loved family, noticed dresses, and signed with a left hand. He was so far away, but maybe ... just maybe ... one day she'd meet him in person. She might even ask him to dance with her, once they were married and that was okay to do, of course.

Is it okay to dance with a boy once he becomes a husband? Rosalee wondered as she drifted off to sleep.

CHAPTER 7

Cars and Gravel

It would be weeks before Rosalee returned to her desk to write Melvin because her family was moving once again. She didn't like to move, especially because of one particular move when she was thirteen, a few years earlier. She would never, ever forget *that day*.

Charles had taught Rosalee how to drive at a young age. It's what parents did in the 1940s. "All young ladies need to learn to manage a car," he'd say to her. Rosalee slid behind the steering wheel, and off they went down the lonely road, across fields sometimes, driving aimlessly to nowhere, just so she could learn to "manage." He was a good instructor, and she listened and learned well. Rosalee could turn on a dime, and she had quite a heavy foot on the pedal, but she was cautious and careful.

"All marks of a good driver," her dad told her.

"Thanks, Dad." Rosalee smiled as she replied and kept her eyes straight ahead.

When Rosalee was behind the wheel, the world seemed completely under her control. Windows down, hair blowing in the wind, and gorgeous sunlight reflecting off the hood of the car, she knew that driving was one of the last steps before becoming a grown woman! Yes, driving was as fun as licking ice cream cones, and she was quite good at doing both!

However, on one certain day when the family was moving, Rosalee was allowed to drive for the journey. Her mother and dad were in the car with her, with Dad in the front and Mom in the back. Dad was a little sleepy, Mom was humming a tune, and Rosalee didn't notice a spread of gravel on the side of the road. She and her dad had never driven on this stretch of road, and she hadn't been warned of any dangers of tires and gravel together. Rosalee swerved just a little, lost control, and the last thing she remembered was running down the street yelling, "I killed my mom! I killed my mom!"

There had been a tool box in the back of the car that had become dislodged when the car swerved, and that box hit Lina in the head. It was the most traumatic experience Rosalee had ever gone through, and she soon became thankful that her mom was alive and well. The scare of that gravel, her mom's voice, and the bruises on her sweet mom's face never left Rosalee … *ever*.

This is why she did not want to move, or to drive while moving, ever again. She liked where they lived, and she was sad to say goodbye to friends. She sat in the back seat while Charles Sr. drove the family away to Austin, just a few miles up the road.

Would Austin have a square for people watching?

Would Lovey come and visit?

What about a soda fountain?

These were important questions that needed a definite answer.

CHAPTER 8

First Date

After months of corresponding back and forth—Rosalee penning about her activities during the days and weekends and her latest sewing projects, and Melvin writing mostly about his family and rations that he didn't care for—Melvin arrived back on the homeland. He then decided to ask Rosalee out on a real date.

By now, Rosalee was old enough for dates with boys. They had to be nice young men, well-mannered, church-going, and have a good and stable future in sight in order for Charles Sr. and Lina to give the much-needed approval Rosalee so longed for. Melvin met all of the criteria on their unwritten list of qualifications for potential husbands, so it was okay if he wanted to show up at her door and knock. And she was certainly hoping he would!

Actually, Melvin was quite shy in person. He wrote well, asked great questions, and was very interesting in his letters, but in person, he was socially awkward, especially around girls. Once Rosalee realized this shyness, she didn't really care for it. And on the day he sent his younger sister to Rosalee's front door to knock and ask if she'd go on a date with Melvin, well, Rosalee almost said no.

"Why can't he ask me himself?" she queried to Vernalee.

Vernalee sweetly replied, "He's just a little backward in the dating department. He has been off to war for a while, you know."

Rosalee was a reasonable girl, and that was a reasonable answer, so she acquiesced and went out with Melvin.

"Moody Melvin" is what she dubbed this young soldier, and "Rosy Lee" was what he dubbed her because she often rubbed a good amount of rosy rouge on her cheeks when they went out for fun. One thing Rosalee could not tolerate was when Melvin stayed in the car instead of coming in to visit her parents. *What was that all about?* Oh well, he was moody, she thought.

Their first date was down at a little hamburger and ice cream stand in Austin, called Sandy's. They didn't know that Sandy's food stand would still be around seventy years later, when they were much older, but it was. The food was that good. Melvin and Rosalee enjoyed one of the burgers there and then, of course, and an ice cream cone. That first date was so memorable. Rosalee loved going out (any reason to wear a new dress), and Melvin loved food, especially hamburgers. They both loved ice cream and found that connecting and talking and looking at people while there at Sandy's was quite an enjoyable evening together.

Sandy's didn't have inside seating. They just had picnic tables out back where people gathered on warm nights to lick their ice cream cones or bite into their juicy hamburgers while the warm breeze blew and the sun set on the day. It was one of those places in the center of town that invited young couples to enjoy a meal surrounded by good smells and good people in a good spot.

"Look at that tree over there," Melvin said as he pointed to a pecan tree in the field behind where they were sitting. "I'm going to have one like that one day in my own yard," he added as he winked at Rosalee's pretty face.

"I love pecans," Rosalee added to the conversation. "I have this amazing pie recipe that tastes as good as you can imagine!" She shyly winked back.

One night, Rosalee fell asleep thinking about Melvin and his moody ways. However, he was a man who loved family, he had served his country well, he always told the truth, and he talked about God and how He took care of him while overseas. So he sure sounded like a good man to marry, perhaps. One time his plane almost went down, and Melvin prayed, and God rescued him *and* saved his life! What a story that would be to tell their children … if they got married … and if they had a boy or a girl, or both! And what if they built a house and planted a pecan tree and she made pecan pies …

Oh, that would be glorious!

CHAPTER 9

Yes

Melvin did ask. In fact, he asked alone, without his sister's help. And Rosalee said yes, although one week prior to the proposal, she had threatened to meet up with good ole' Darrell again. It wasn't a real fight with Melvin, per se; it was just that Rosalee often didn't understand Melvin's insensitivity to her needs, and she thought maybe she could make him jealous enough to shape up. It never worked, and there she was in his arms, looking into his twinkling eyes of adoration, saying, "Yes, I'll marry you!"

She kissed his lips and felt his strong arms pull her close. It was a good thing Charles Sr. never saw that kiss. Rosalee was sure there was something so wrong with kissing a boy, but she just couldn't help herself with Melvin. At least they weren't kissing in the water, wearing bathing suits. They were sitting on a rock in a park, in full daylight.

CHAPTER 10

I Do

Rosalee didn't wear a long, flowy, white wedding gown. Many of the girls wore fitted suits for their weddings during those years, so that's what Rosalee wore as well. And wow, did she look sharp. It was perfectly form-fitting, and although she was late to the wedding ... she did show up and say, "I do."

It was 5:00 p.m., time for the wedding to begin, on November 2, 1946. Rosalee and Melvin had invited friends and family to gather as they made their vows and started their life together as man and wife.

Melvin had looked around and asked his friends, "Where is Rosalee?" and no one knew.

But Rosalee was once again on the side of the road. Not in a bed of gravel, but finding herself with no gas. Once she arrived, that began years of being late wherever she went and years of Melvin wondering why she was so late—so much so that they arrived in separate cars to most of the places they went!

Her wedding attire was navy and gold in color, and she stood beside her military man as they cut the cake—the first of many cakes—and made their vows. Vows were important;

they both knew that. They had both committed their lives to loving God, and now they were promising to love each other in all of those situations in life, like sickness and health, in richness and poorness. Rosalee had no idea how hard that would be, to still love, even when life was hard … as it was sure to be.

The seats were full, and the people from the church gathered to see this match made in heaven, or rather on a bench while eating a juicy burger cut in half, for two. There was no dancing, only a little light music as the two walked hand in hand down the aisle after the last promise of a life together forever.

Melvin and Rosalee settled into married life easily enough. He landed a job with the Austin Police Force, initially writing tickets to illegally parked drivers. And it wasn't too long before Rosalee was pregnant with their first child.

CHAPTER 11

Sometimes ... Tomatoes

Rosalee was often fearful with Melvin working the police beat, especially when he moved to a more dangerous position. But she often gave thanks at night, when she was alone with her thoughts, that he wasn't a preacher. She didn't really like being a PK (preacher's kid) at all. Her dad was often heckled and mistreated at those tent meetings in town. Sometimes people even threw tomatoes at him because they didn't like what he was preaching.

One particular night, a man who attended the meeting asked Charles for a ride home in the horse and buggy. But, because Charles had preached about how the Lord will "direct your paths," the man refused to tell Charles where he lived.

"Just ask God to tell you," he sneered as he sat squarely on the seat next to Charles and waited for him to move forward. "Let that Holy Ghost show up and whisper where I live," he said.

And one other time, Charles had two men mistreat him so badly with teasing and bullying. However, because of Charles's kindness, those mean men asked Charles to stop so they could pray and be saved and be rid of all their sins.

Rosalee knew that was a good story in the end, but the bad stories of the preacher's life seemed to outweigh all the good ones. It was not fun to watch her dad be criticized for his faith, and it hurt her heart ... badly.

Charles also became very depressed with his congregations as he pastored small churches in between those tent meetings. If things weren't going well, he even threatened to end his life.

Once, Rosalee had to stand by the bathroom door and call to her dad, "Please come out, Daddy. We need you."

With enough coaxing and pleading, he emerged with tears on his cheeks and hugged his daughter, and she breathed a sigh of relief, until the next time. There was even this one incident where Charles took the whole family into the woods and made threats that scared Rosalee to the bone. He was completely spent, exhausted, and overwrought with the frustrations of people and congregations and rules and tents, so he thought it best to end it all for his entire family. Rosalee grew to fear those times, which rarely occurred. But she knew that the life of a preacher must be similar to the life of a soldier in combat—never knowing when one was going to be shot at, trampled over, or left to die.

Thank goodness Melvin was home from the war! And though he was a policeman, that job had to be better than being a preacher. No, being a preacher was not a good profession, and she was thankful daily that Melvin was an officer of the law instead. He did look fine in his uniform, now that the Air Force one was hung in the back of the closet. Melvin was tall and had a sweet smile that warmed her heart.

She was proud of their little life they were starting to enjoy as a married couple, now one in spirit and in flesh ...

CHAPTER 12

Top Three

Church.
God.
Heaven.

Those words were so familiar to Rosalee. The church was most important. It had to be or else why would her dad cry so when the people weren't making up a good congregation? It was also where God was talked about and preached about and praised out loud, so that's why God came in second place. Heaven was this place she had heard about, with streets of gold and no sorrow and no night, but one only got there if one repented.

"When would everyone get to see heaven?" she once asked her dad after a sermon where he'd talked about streets of gold and pearly gates.

"In the sweet by and by," he answered. They sang a song by that title at almost every service.

However, Rosalee liked another song called "Stepping on the Clouds," probably because she loved all of the cloud pictures she and her brother had seen together. Stepping on top of cloud rainbows and cloud bunnies and cloud sharks while angels were fanning their wings beside her did seem inviting. One day ... she could just imagine it. She also wondered what kind of fashion ladies wore in heaven.

Melvin wasn't a preacher, but he made sure they were in church, in the second row, every time the doors were open. It felt like the right thing to do; it seemed to secure them a spot "up there," and prayer took place, which always helped Rosalee feel better. Talking to God was great because she knew He listened and cared. That was one thing she felt was a right thing, something she had learned while under the tents as a child. Prayer could bring about miracles, peace, and all sorts of joy ... so praying she did.

After Raetta was born (she was named after Melvin's middle name, Rae, and an aunt named Mary Etta), the threesome of Melvin, Rosalee, and baby became churchgoers who never missed a day. Missing church had to be a sin, Rosalee was sure of it. So she made sure the family was dressed to go to the meetings at least three times a week. However, Melvin's police job required him to work some on Sundays. The holy day! The day when they were supposed to be glued to the pew, intently listening to sermons and songs.

Missing Sunday service was a huge no-no for Melvin, who had learned to follow rules as a young boy, and then more-so when he entered the armed services. It wasn't long before Melvin found another job at a bank. It suited him just fine. He hung up yet another uniform in favor of a pressed shirt and tie under a jacket with matching slacks.

Besides his job at the bank, Melvin also had heard the call.

That's what it was named back then when someone felt this pull and urge, heard this *voice*, to preach the Word.

"How can this be happening?" Rosalee questioned when

Melvin let her know that he'd made the decision to work at the bank full-time and preach the Word too.

"It's what I promised to God, to serve Him faithfully," Melvin replied sternly, as if to say that the discussion was over.

Now, they had a young daughter in the mix. How could he fit this in, and how could she possibly endure the life of a preacher's wife, a PW? Rosalee felt panicked and heartbroken.

Certainly, being a preacher's wife must be even worse than a preacher's daughter!

CHAPTER 13

The Call

Rosalee sat at the same desk where she'd first read the letter from Melvin, only this time the desk was in the bedroom they shared together. It was against a wall, right by a window where the morning sun shone in and illuminated dust particles that floated in the air like little tiny snowflakes (as she imagined what snowflakes might be like). She had been drawn to Melvin first because he was a lefty soldier; then she adored him in his starched khakis and even loved the look of his suits he wore to work. But a preacher? It couldn't be that God was calling her husband to be the brunt of hecklers, the worrisome teacher, or the man who was "led by the Spirit" into all truths. Rosalee loved God, but she didn't love this news … no, not at all. She could not bear the image in her head of her husband standing behind a pulpit (the stand where preachers stood with their Bible laid open in front of them), and she let Melvin know.

"I don't want to be married to a preacher!" she exclaimed.

And then Melvin reminded her of that rescue when his plane was about to go down and he cried out to God. He made a promise to serve Him however He saw fit if he landed safely at home.

Rosalee replied, "But I didn't make that promise!"

Rosalee stood up from the desk and exited the bedroom. She walked to her sewing machine in the corner of the living room and felt the fabric spread out to be cut. Tears fell down her cheeks because it was as if she'd received a death sentence for a crime she hadn't committed or a life sentence to the confines of the cell of a preacher's wife. But soon she wiped her tears, began cutting across the grain, let down her defenses, and breathed …

"Hopefully, life will be different with Melvin," she prayed. "Hopefully, life will be different …"

As the scissors glided effortlessly through the floral print laid before her, Rosalee saw again the images of flying tomatoes hitting her dad in the head—the red juice and seeds running down his white shirt, against his black suit. She thought of all the rules, including "no swimming" and "only wear dresses," and wondered what new rules Melvin would now apply to her as his dutiful wife. She wondered again about the Holy Ghost and His direction, as Melvin had mentioned it to her. How did He direct Melvin and not speak to Rosalee about it first? And finally, she wept tears that dotted the material like raindrops on a windshield, drops that didn't run but only soaked in deep. She saw herself at the door, possibly pleading with Melvin when the congregation disappointed him and God. Fear gripped her tightly around the neck, and she felt as if she were choking … choking for air and choking from crying.

This must be what it feels like to be drowning in a swimming pool where girls are not supposed to be, Rosalee thought.

Melvin sat in the bedroom, studying, unaware of the tears that she cried. He had heard the call and was answering it right now as his first sermon was coming together ... and Rosalee's world was falling apart.

CHAPTER 14

Focus

It had been an especially hard year for Charles and Lina, Rosalee's parents. The furniture store was no longer bringing in income. People were buying new tables and chairs at fancy stores in town. The church where Rosalee's dad pastored suffered from a lack of attendance, and there was constant frustration with Charles's "other" family. He had been married once before and had a daughter too, only that daughter was much older than Rosalee and Charlie. In fact, she was never spoken of. Myrtle was their half-sister, but she was fully out of the picture. Rosalee didn't really know why her dad divorced his first wife, but she knew it was quite a scandal. And she never really understood why Myrtle hated her dad so. To Rosalee, Charles Sr. was the most kind-hearted man she'd ever known.

"God, I don't want the life I had as a little girl," Rosalee prayed the best she knew how.

Prayer, to her, was petitioning God for answers and then waiting to see if He would actually do what she asked. And somehow, deep in the recesses of her heart, Rosalee knew that God heard her and would grant her the strength to live as a preacher's wife, with the memories of her dad and her half-sister and all of the tomatoes and their juices in tow—if that's what she needed to do.

Wiping her eyes with a nearby scrap of discarded material, Rosalee stood up to make dinner, call Raetta over to the table and set a plate for the three of them. They ate in silence that night after bowing their heads to offer thanks for the food that was nourishment to their bodies.

"Amen," Melvin ended the prayer with resolve, and Rosalee looked at him with a nod, as together they would face this life that was familiar to her … and a new adventure to him.

Did he know what he had signed up for?

Would he be able to stand when others didn't?

Didn't he realize he was entering a jungle full of scary people and dark places?

Rosalee was sure that her husband had no idea of the life to come, except standing up to tell others of the good news of Jesus Christ. Just what was that good news? She wondered. Oh yes, it was that Jesus died and rose again, clearing us all of wrongdoings and giving us hope for a future. She would focus on that hope of a future—a good one.

Yes, that would be her focus and her resolve.

CHAPTER 15

Kids and Clothes

Melvin and Rosalee had two more children after Raetta. Six years later, a son was born. And three and a half years after that, another girl. Rosalee wanted five children, and she actually carried five but only held on to three. Mom, Dad, and three kids would be their family to raise and to love, together. Rosalee continued to sew and design clothes that were the envy of all of her friends. Raetta and Marcy had the finest clothes with the cutest attention to detail—outfits that could have easily been featured in *Vogue Magazine*, had any photographer dared to snap and enter them. Color, pattern, and flair—the Clearman family stepped out in the best when they went to church three times a week, with extra services on Fridays ... sometimes.

It was fun for Rosalee—an escape and a treat, to shop for patterns and fabric. She continued to have an eye for style and the ability to see that one sleeve of a pattern would look pretty on the bodice of another pattern. And that would all connect to the skirt of an entirely different one! Butterick, McCall, and Vogue. Marcy often went with her mom to choose the patterns. It was great fun for both of them, picking out a creation, unique and one-of-a kind. Rosalee had found her outlet, expertise, and a place to be creative to the best of her abilities. And her daughters loved wearing what their mother turned out.

"Mom, look at this pattern!" Marcy often pointed as they sat on small stools and flipped through the pages of huge pattern books.

"Oh, Marcy, I love that. It will look perfect on you," Rosalee replied as they rose and walked down the aisles and found just the right fabric and colors for the new creation to come.

One Easter Sunday, the entire family entered a parade at the one shopping center in town, Hancock. Each family wore their Sunday best outfits, which often included hats and white gloves on the ladies, black suits and ties with pressed white shirts on the men. They walked around the center as judges looked on. There were going to be prizes given out, and to their surprise, the Clearman family won "Best Dressed!" Rosalee beamed with excitement, as she had never won anything before in her life—except once when she was employee of the month at Woolworth's soda fountain, where she worked for a time. She was granted a coupon for a chocolate milkshake on the house. But "Best Dressed!" It was as if she had been handed a gold medal at the Olympics. Another time, Rosalee sewed together an all-American outfit: a beautiful red, white, and blue dress for Marcy. It too won an award in a local contest. Marcy wore the cotton flag dress with her navy loafers and stood proudly as each contestant appeared in front of the panel. She too was amazed at her mom's creativity and talent!

Rosalee's creations were noticed, her family was beautiful, and she was so happy to be a part of both.

Sewing was it.

While Melvin worked at the bank during the day and shut the bedroom door to study for sermons at night, Rosalee snipped, sewed, and pressed. She created what her imagination saw and then placed it on her girls when the creations were complete. She crafted really cute shift dresses for her older daughter. These were sleeveless straight-lined dresses, and she chose the most colorful of fabrics. After all, it was the '60s. Even tent dresses were all the rage. These were dresses that started out fitted at the top and then widened as they hit the knees—thus the name "tent dress!" Her kids were growing up as PKs, and she often prayed they wouldn't be harmed in the way she was. Their religion banned pants, so dresses they all wore, even to church camp in the summer, where girls were required to play sports. Rosalee and her girls never understood these mandates, but that's where they lived and what they had to do while Melvin preached and served and pastored the church where they attended.

CHAPTER 16

Swimming

Rosalee never learned to swim as a child because of the swimsuit rule, and she never went fishing with Melvin because of the pants rule. Swimsuits were too revealing. And fishing in a dress? Well, how could that be sensible? Oh, Melvin wanted her to go with him to the banks where he set up camp and threw in his line. He invited her to fish with him, but she refused unless she could wear pants. The children wanted their parents to swim with them the few times they were allowed in a pool (on vacation), and one, and only one, time Melvin went in the water with them. But it was just not right, to show one's legs in the water with the opposite sex or to wear form-fitting pants that hugged too tightly to curves. Swimming became fun for the children, at least a little, but Rosalee only sat and watched, thinking up the next outfit she'd design.

And the next week, Melvin asked, "Come fishing with me."

Rosalee replied for the umpteenth time, "Not in a dress."

On that one vacation (that the family took once a year because it was just wrong to miss church more than two Sundays a year), Melvin got in the motel pool. The kids

weren't sure why, but it sure was fun, and then it was over ...
never to happen again. Rosalee absolutely loved vacation
because she enjoyed getting away from preacher life and the
busyness of home life. And she enjoyed the sun and especially
the moon when they were out away from the city, just the five
of them. Each vacation, the entire family was like five birds
that were uncaged to fly for a bit away from their closed
doors, their daily food and water, into the beauty of the sky
and the wonder out there just waiting to be enjoyed. She often
recalled those sailing ships her brother Charlie had seen in the
sky and imagined herself on one of them on the ocean blue ...

More often than not, Rosalee packed potato chip
sandwiches for the trips. And the recipe for one such sandwich
is just this:

White bread slathered with mayonnaise (actually, Miracle
Whip) with potato chips piled up between.

Ruffles were the best. There was nothing crunchier or
tastier because it was living life on the edge. On the edge of
the road, that is, away from rules and meetings and into a
little freedom and fun.

Melvin pulled over to a nice spot for stopping. The girls
donned scarves tied under their chins if it was windy. Rosalee
opened the tin box, in which she had packed their lunch, and
everyone grabbed a sandwich. There were no worries about
the fat in the mayo, the oil on the chips, or whether or not
the bread was wheat or white. It was surely white, and these
sandwiches were awfully tasty.

Fisher's Court was a place the family frequented on
vacation, a place with a pool for the kids to swim. Somehow,
it was okay for them to swim there, even if other kids showed
up, but these PKs were never allowed in a public pool back
home. Rosalee often wondered about these unexplained rules

for here and not there, but she had learned as a child to just stay quiet and mutter her misgivings under her breath.

"What would it be like to learn to swim?" she wondered out loud as she watched the kids splash and squeal with delight in the cool water on a hot summer day.

But oh so quickly, the family was back home and back to church three times a week, and the thoughts of swimming were long gone. Maybe one day she'd venture into the water with the kids … but probably not.

Swimming pools were only for dreaming about, and fishing by the lake was only for arguing about … until next summer rolled around again, and the car was filled with laughter and the sound of crunchy potato chip bites at a roadside stop once again.

CHAPTER 17

Phone Work

Rosalee didn't make any income sewing, so she began selling *TV Guide Magazine* for a little extra cash. *TV Guide* was a magazine that listed all of the shows on television and gave the times they were showing on each channel. She was great at selling because she didn't mind if people told her no. She just dialed the next number.

"Hello, this is Rosalee," she'd start out with that sweet voice that made people want to listen further. "I'm selling a great magazine that you will want in your home ..."

And then a sale was made, and another, and another ...

Rosalee was like that: determined and strong. She became quite good at her job, which would later be called telemarketing. The kids were active in church with their friends, involved in school and extracurricular activities. And Melvin was still preaching and working at the bank. A banker *and* a preacher—never a good combo, so she'd heard. Rosalee was still somewhat disappointed that her police-wife status had been demoted (at least that's how she saw it) to a preacher's-wife status. Both PWs, both dangerous, and the latter not what she wanted.

It wasn't that Rosalee hated church ... or God. She actually loved both, but not with Melvin at the helm of what she'd grown up to see as a sinking ship. And she'd never learned how to swim ... and couldn't—unless of course, she wore a dress!

When Rosalee's two younger children were teens, they actually submitted a proposal to the board of directors for their church organization to change the rules about girls wearing dresses to summer camp. The brother and sister duo had to be especially careful about their wording, careful not to offend the higher-ups and to make their case for the absurdity of girls playing sports in dresses. It was a celebration and a victory for all of the girls in churches around the area when it was finally agreed that girls could wear loose-fitting pantsuits on days when there were sports on the agenda at summer camp. Pantsuits on the baseball field in the middle of a Texas summer was as good as they could get. It was a victory, nonetheless.

The phone work became good work, with Rosalee's list of subscribers becoming full and long. She was on her way to developing her own career apart from filling a seat in a church building, nodding at every word from the front. She even paid the two younger kids to look up phone numbers in those huge books of all the people who lived in the city and beyond. They were paid one penny per number, and both Marcy and Bo became quite quick with their eyes and their hands, and offered up long lists in a short amount of time! Then Rosalee called those numbers, and Rosalee sold, and Rosalee prospered.

It wouldn't be long before Rosalee's determination, will to work, and desire to bless her family paid off. Her little business of selling one lone magazine turned into a big business of selling all magazines to people and school libraries across the world. Her kids had sold the idea of sensibility to the masses. And she might not be swimming in a river of water, but she was certainly swimming in a pool of success. She wasn't afraid of drowning—no, not at all. In fact, she was completely happy in her office that was built onto the back of the house, where she hired several employees, set up multiple computers (in later years), and made customer service her priority.

CHAPTER 18

PW

Life as a preacher's wife was lonely. Rosalee did have a few close friends—one lady in particular, but that didn't last long. Somehow, preachers' wives had lots of expectations to fulfill just because their husbands were pastors. It didn't matter that Rosalee never felt or heard the call; she was expected to answer it right alongside the one who did. There were long hours with Melvin working at the bank as a loan officer and then coming home to study for sermons, night after night, week after week. In order to cope, feel good about herself, and delight in something that was just for her, she worked long hours as well ... especially as the kids got older. She quite enjoyed early mornings and late nights at her desk in front of her computer, where she'd become quite adept at answering emails and writing them to customers she'd come to know on a first name basis.

Rosalee went to church, sat, and listened to sermons, and then did it all over again, every Wednesday night, Sunday morning, and Sunday night. One of the best things she loved about going to church, aside from the singing (she and Melvin both loved the singing!) was the fact that it was a place to go where she could get dressed up! And dressed up she was. She often wore dresses with perfectly matching jewelry and heels that completed the outfit, and she looked rather smart in that trio of loveliness! Her children were her life, as she catered to every need they had ... but they too were growing up into their own interests and lives.

CHAPTER 19

Lake Time

Some days, Rosalee was just sad, lonely, and not quite sure where she fit in among her family, church, and community. Her job with the magazines became her lifeline to identity and worth. However, she envied the couples who were out on the weekend, occasionally at the lake (including Melvin's siblings), enjoying time with family. Melvin's family enjoyed fishing and boating and all things out on the water, but Rosalee never experienced that sort of fun. She just watched it from the shore, the few times they ventured out (on a Saturday, of course) to be with them all.

"Come on into the boat, Rosalee," one of Melvin's sisters-in-law asked.

"Not this time," Rosalee replied, although she knew there'd probably never be a time.

She really wanted to, but she just couldn't, so she always politely declined every time the family gathered by the lake. No one knew that Rosalee had never learned to swim. And of course, the family had to be back for church on Sunday, so their visits were never long. Her kids did get in the boat and even learned to ski a little because swimming in the water with family was okay. It wasn't evil or unholy, she supposed, because it was family time.

Rosalee heard the kids talk of how fun it was out on the boat with the wind blowing against their tanned faces. She heard them squeal with delight about how they got up on their skis the first time and how they hit a wave and then, *splash*, they fell into the water. The boat had to turn around and come back to pick them up. She was so happy that the kids were having fun, and she didn't wish too much for fun like that. She'd learned to sit in her cute skirts and matching tops up by the lake house, preparing the potato salad and sandwiches for the hungry skiers once they hit land again. That too was fun, so she concentrated on making the best of it.

Over time, with the bitterness and sadness she felt, and the fact that she was alone in her thoughts, Rosalee bickered with Melvin. It was often bickering over family time.

"Why do you pout when we go out to see a play?" she asked Melvin because it just wasn't fun when he folded his arms in disgust throughout the evening.

Silence. There was no answer.

They didn't go to the movies, but once in a while, a play was on the calendar. Although the difference between the two was never understood in Rosalee's mind or in the minds of the kids.

"Why do I only hear news and personal communication when you're speaking to the congregation?" she queried when they arrived home after a Sunday morning service where Melvin announced to everyone how much he appreciated his wife.

She wanted to be told that personally, on a real date, in the dark after the sunset, with his eyes looking into hers ... maybe even near a body of water ... or actually out on the water in a boat, with the wind blowing her hair.

CHAPTER 20

Gone

One huge event took place when Rosalee and Melvin's eldest daughter decided to marry a guy from California and move two thousand miles away to live by an entirely different body of water, the Pacific Ocean. She would say goodbye to the Gulf Coast forever. *This one change ominously began drowning Rosalee, to where she could barely breathe, even though she'd never stepped foot from the cold sand into the deep blue.* How could she make it without her daughter nearby? Melvin too was upset that a young man they barely knew was "taking" their daughter away. He was angry; she was disappointed and sad; and now their family of five was a family decreased by one.

How was Rosalee going to come up for air without a lifesaver?

Even if someone threw her a ring, she wouldn't know how to float or kick her feet, so maybe she really would sink into the deep, deep darkness, never to be seen again.

Oh, that must be what it's like to drown, she thought as her daughter flew away the day after the wedding.

Her firstborn was gone.

CHAPTER 21

Only Four

Rosalee remembered when her own brother went off to war and the sadness that settled over her parents' eyes—a sadness that dimmed the light in their family of four. Four bright lamps had been shining in their home, illuminating the doors and windows, but it was suddenly decreased to three when her brother was transported across the world. All sorts of corners in the house grew dark and dreary, and home wasn't a fun place to be with just three.

It was the same darkness now, only it was four instead of five. Melvin, Rosalee and the two younger children were left at home while the eldest daughter made her way into a new life with her husband, far from her mom. Rosalee cried. Melvin grieved. And both retreated to the familiar routine of bank and church, magazines and sewing. It was a well-oiled machine by now, this life of the Clearman family, one that could run in the dark if it had to, without a squeak in any joint.

The girl once too poor to be a famous designer was now a grown woman with funds—a mother and a wife. But one child was gone, and life had to go on.

Rosalee emerged from the sadness by giving away those funds that she was earning. It was her way of staving off the loneliness of missing her daughter while learning to thrive and survive with her now family of four. She knew all moms experienced sadness when their children left home, but it didn't matter that she knew. She'd been a mom to her eldest for twenty-two years, and now motherhood was changing for her.

What am I becoming?

She often thought about what life would be like when her other two left, and she began to carve out a path for herself that included giving away that which she had to bless others who had not.

CHAPTER 22

Giving

One young girl moved to the United States from Central America and began attending Rosalee and Melvin's church as she was engaged to a young man there. Yes, Rosalee now called church her place too, as she did indeed love the people who came week after week to hear her husband preach. They were kind people, and she grew to love them all. Even though she still felt church was mostly Melvin's thing, Rosalee sat up, listened, and observed the people who came and went. It was much like she used to do as a young girl, when she sat on the square with her friend, watching ladies walk by in their new hats and shoes. Only this young girl showed up a bit afraid, with her big bright eyes and her thin frame, as she was about to begin a new life away from her mom too. She was marrying one of the boys in the church.

Rosalee placed some cash into the young girl's hand and said, "Here. Go buy a dress … any dress."

Rosalee knew the value and the lift that comes from something new to wear and how it brightens the countenance and lightens the soul, so she gave generously, without a thought of remorse or regret. She could not wait to see what this young girl picked out as Rosalee released the funds into the hands of this newcomer. It felt good, releasing that cash. It felt so good that it would become part of who Rosalee was: an extravagant giver to those in need. And it healed a part of the heart that was broken and empty and filled it with joy.

That release was like a stroke of the arm into the water, a passage through dark seas, and arrival to the other side, away from grief and sadness of loss. Rosalee was breathless with the air that escaped her lungs as she walked away, knowing she'd obeyed and given. She'd learned one of the greatest joys in life. She emerged out of the water onto the sandy beach, where the sun felt good on her skin and in her soul.

And yet, she never really swam a stroke at all.

CHAPTER 23

The Exodus

The business of magazine selling grew, and Rosalee began hiring employees to fill the chairs in her office, now bustling with activity, phone calls, typewriter and keyboard clicks, and file drawers opening and closing. The business of church was waxing and waning, with people coming and going— sometimes more going than coming. And as people came in with needs, what Rosalee gave was received; and her heart grew larger.

Every time a new family arrived at Trinity Chapel promising to serve and to give, another one left over some grievance or disappointment in the way church was going or what the pastor was saying or for no good reason at all. Rosalee watched from the vantage point of the sixth seat from the front, where her husband preached week after week.

Not long after her eldest had married, an exodus took place in the church, much akin to the exodus from Egypt; it left Rosalee and Melvin in a quandary, for sure. It wasn't an exodus from slavery into the Promised Land, but it was an experience that neither had ever had before. You see, with Melvin working at the bank and pastoring, there were some who didn't agree with that division of allegiance. There were others who demanded that a new building be raised so the church could grow. Ideas were voiced, disagreements ensued, and one by one, individuals and families left. Accusations were made; and after all was said and done, there was a skeleton crew left to run this once-thriving congregation.

However, the skeleton crew grew skins and bones again because the two younger children stepped up to the plate to fill the shoes of their leaders and friends that had gone. The son became the worship leader and the daughter played the organ and led the youth group; because it was expected and there were holes to be filled. There was no time for counseling or therapy for these two, although they sure could have used it. They had both been in the choir, served in the youth group, sat in the seats and worshiped with the masses. But now they were leading in every capacity there was, at very young ages. It didn't seem like there was any other choice because the church had to go on ... and it did.

It was like that well-oiled machine, now with a few loose bolts—but ones not visible to anyone, even to this family of four.

Rosalee was sad. Hadn't Melvin given his all and done his best to serve these people? Her daughters were upset at the upheaval as well and quite enjoyed scribbling on the faces of each one who'd left (in the church directory). The eldest had flown in for a visit to be with her family during this crisis.

Rosalee had flashbacks of the tomatoes that were thrown hard at her own dad's face as he preached on the side of the road to hoboes and gypsies.

Smack!

Right between the eyes as the red juice ran down her father's shaven chin, as if he'd been cut open and wounded.

Only this time, it was her husband who'd been the target of mistrust, misunderstanding, and judgment from the people he served. Rosalee could feel the juice running down her own face as the sting of friends gone and the reality of church life hit her in the face once again. In fact, those tomatoes left their stain on the cheeks of the entire family ... the youngest daughter especially. She really didn't want anything to do with church people because they had left her family holding the reins of wild horses she didn't know how to tame.

A pastor's wife wasn't the life Rosalee had wanted, not at all.

So why was it hers to bear?

Back home, she again withdrew to her office, eased into the comfort of her black chair with a tall back, and began communicating with her clients: the ones who paid and the ones she served. They all appreciated her good service, and so good service they would get. In fact, Rosalee was determined that good service would always be what her company was known for. Not one tomato anywhere in sight. She would make sure of it.

Working was her escape, her retreat, and her resource for all good things to be had and to give away.

CHAPTER 24

No Rest

By now, Rosalee had stewed, stammered, and solicited help for her loneliness, sadness, and isolation that she felt as the pastor's wife. Pastors' wives at that time were expected to lead the women's ministry (to where? she often wondered) of the church. However, this was not Rosalee's cup of tea, as she'd rather be sewing or selling. She was good at both of those things! Pastors' wives were expected to show up, sit quietly, and serve constantly, as there was "no rest for the weary in the work of the Lord," she'd heard somewhere. In fact, she found herself quoting it to her own children, even though she didn't like that phrase.

Where had she learned it? It must have been what she'd heard under a tent somewhere in the middle of town on a hot summer's night, as the people sat and listened with their fans in hand to the sermon from the front.

Work from sun up to sun down,
and show up at church in the town,
that was what made life go round and round ...

Once, Rosalee even considered leaving her husband and family, as rejection and loneliness almost pushed her out the door of her home and church. She sought counsel and was even encouraged to leave, but she didn't. She loved Melvin and her children so much. So much that it often hurt. Melvin kept preaching, and the two kids kept serving, until one day ... they also both married and left.

And then there were two.

CHAPTER 25

The Routine

Rosalee was now home alone: no more clothes to sew, no one to shuttle back and forth to school, no one to shoulder her pain, and no one to laugh with over supper. The kids had so often made her laugh, especially when they used to trick their older sister just before sitting down to a meal. The family gathered around a long bar, where Rosalee lined up the dishes, and everyone served themselves. Her son Bo removed his older sister's chair when she stood up to fill her plate, and then when she sat down ... well ... she landed on the floor. The older sister didn't laugh, the younger two were scolded, and dinner was then eaten. Sometimes, the family lingered at a bigger table to play a card game of Rook, and that too was fun. And once in a while, the family knelt around the bed together at night for a small family devotional before bed. But all three kids were gone now, a normal part of parenthood for a mom to experience for sure, but a harder than normal experience for Rosalee.

The clicking of the typewriter keys became her rhythm to each day by which she moved and breathed. The only songs left in her heart were those tunes from the 1940s about apple trees and love. Sometimes, Melvin caught her eye and smiled as she hummed the familiar tune.

Melvin and Rosalee continued as preacher and preacher's wife, showing up at least three times a week for service. And they stayed married, even sometimes singing "Hand in Hand with Jesus" when asked to do so. She would hold his hand, and he would lift it high as they sang about walking with Him, together. She knew this was truth, holding a higher hand so that she could hold the lower one. So she stood there and never thought about leaving again.

And she kept on working.

Melvin continued to only vacation two weeks out of the year since it was against his religion to miss any more Sundays from church than that. He reiterated that rule often. Two weeks out of the year the family used to vacation with those road trips and potato chips, and now that the kids were all grown, Rosalee and Melvin flew together to the eldest daughter's home in California for their yearly getaways. It was beautiful where her daughter lived, and the weather was much cooler in the summer than in Texas, so it was quite refreshing.

Two weeks out of the year, it was vacation time, but Rosalee still never packed a bathing suit, because swimming was not a part of the life of a pastor's wife. Not even in California … or anywhere.

Church was.

It was like clockwork, that church life she lived. Sometimes, the hands on the clock were loud and evident as people filled the benches in the church building. And other times, the tick-tock was barely audible as people exited once again. But time went on, with Melvin and Rosalee together, in the rhythm that the ticking brought: week after week, month after month, year after year. The second and minute hands made their way around in a circle over and over again.

Melvin told stories from the pulpit and encouraged people to love God with all their hearts. He often recalled that fateful day when his plane almost went down while in the Air Force. Rosalee secretly slipped cash into the hands of more newcomers. And this duo also attended Valentine's banquets, where they were requested to sing that hand song again and again. It warmed the hearts of the listeners to see this aging couple sing together, holding hands. Other couples aspired to be like them, to discover the secret to their "happiness" together after all these years.

Rosalee had a very nice alto voice, and Melvin could barely hold a tune; he didn't have much of a sense of rhythm either. His claps were often off, but they were nevertheless joyful. This one particular song became their anthem, what they were known for, and the lyrics were the glue that kept them from breaking … because they were life to their souls.

Hand in hand we walk each day,
Hand in hand along the way,
Walking thus I cannot stray,
Hand in hand with Jesus

CHAPTER 26

Christmas

Grandkids were now part of the family, and Rosalee had never known such joy. These kids were like empty baskets into which Granny now poured every resource she had. If the kids needed clothes, it wasn't for long because she gave. Birthdays were another chance to give and to lavish. And for no reason at all, the kids received gifts and blessings and food and love, all just because Rosalee's hands were always open, never closed in a fist.

Christmas was the event of the year for Rosalee. She looked forward to it the minute summer was over, and she began to plan for the giving, the wrapping, and the family time with her kids and their kids. The children often heard Rosalee say, "You can't take it with you," (referring to dollars and cents) as she asked for their wish lists, which had to include categories of gifts like books, clothes, home things, and car stuff. She liked to give so that there was a pile of goodies for each person, to fulfill their needs in all areas. And she gave generously, so much that those piles of presents reached tall and wide when the family gathered on Christmas morning. And it took all day to open each one. On Christmas

Eve, the grandchildren gathered to bring in the gifts from the garage, where they had been wrapped and stashed away, waiting to be set just right under the tree in the family den. The eldest grandson, in particular, loved the job of stacking the boxes and gift bags up high and then sitting in a chair to gaze, think about the next morning, and wonder what was inside each treat from Granny.

The youngest daughter was Rosalee's partner in crime when it came to Christmas. They started in September with the wish lists of what each person wanted, and they organized and shopped, until on Black Friday they finished, enjoying every crowded store and every long line. It really was the most fun for both of them! Rosalee enjoyed this time with her daughter because they both absolutely loved shopping. Shopping was a pastime like no other as they walked the aisles together, each pushing a cart and talking over each outfit, each toy, or each gadget for this person and that one. There was always a stop for lunch as they regrouped and analyzed their lists. And then they were off for another full afternoon of buying and smiling.

When it came time to start wrapping, Rosalee and her daughter sat in the living room of Rosalee's house (the room where kids were not allowed because it was the one room that was kept perfect!) And they cut and they taped, and they wrapped and they tagged, all with Christmas music playing in the background. Each year, they decided on a way to designate gifts, instead of with nametags. One year, everyone had their gifts wrapped in their own individual paper, and another year the faces of each family member were printed and affixed to each gift! It was such fun digging for their gifts among the mountain before them!

When Christmas morning arrived, the entire family

gathered and made sure Granny had her special spot where she could see each person open each gift. It was the most joyful day of the year for her.

She absolutely loved every, "This was just what I wanted!" or "Thank you, Granny!"

She even loved the little ones, as one once commented, "Panty hose? Really?" and held up a new pair of tights.

Rosalee and the entire clan enjoyed opening one gift at a time, each one learning to wait their turn and observe what the others received. This was a way for the family to learn about giving, receiving, and observing those around them. It was beautiful, chaotic, and exhausting: all three rolled into a day of joy.

Each girl received an outfit, at least one. And each girl slipped away into another room of the house to try on her new gift and then parade in front of the family as Granny/Mom looked on with admiration, pride, and that thing called joy.

Rosalee enjoyed this day more than the other 364 because her family was together. She had given (her purpose in life) to each one, and she could see the delight on their faces as each present was unwrapped.

She smiled big.

Her heart was full.

She loved giving more than life itself.

It was who she was, this lady who'd learned to rise above the dark waters of the loneliness of church life into the clear pool where she splashed to her heart's content in giving.

Maybe this is what swimming is like, she often wondered. Stepping into a huge pool of water and submersing below while holding your breath—emerging above with a gasp and a smile when you've made it all the way across to the other side. Giving felt like that; it literally took her breath away to make others happy. And it felt like she'd accomplished a great feat as her hands opened and gave again and again ...

CHAPTER 27

Thriving

Rosalee never stopped moving. She was much like the Energizer bunny that used to pop up on television commercials: he too just kept going and going. Melvin was busy with his calling of pastoring the church. Their days of his fishing and her sewing were now his preaching and her selling. They both thrived on watching their grandkids play sports and traveling to see the kids across the country play as well. It became their new connection, their one thing in common that drew them together: the children and their children. They settled into the role of grandparents, and they were both good at grandparenting together.

Melvin churched.

Rosalee gave.

It's how they rolled.

They also focused on family dinners for birthdays. This was a great time to sit down to a meal together, give thanks, and listen to the family chatter. Each event was specially catered to the one whose birthday was being celebrated. The person was invited to pick his or her choice of restaurant, and

Rosalee then asked, "What do you want for your birthday?" as she loved to give.

The family then came around the table and ate to their hearts' content. Even the dessert was picked out by the birthday person, and gifts were exchanged. Everyone left with bellies, and hearts, completely full.

Especially Melvin and Rosalee.

CHAPTER 28

Just a Little

Rosalee had listened to every sermon Melvin preached, and she knew all of his stories by heart. He again shared the story of how he was with his troop during WWII and the plane in which they were flying was struggling to stay in the air. That story everyone knew if they'd ever sat for very long in their church. It was in that moment of fear that he called out to God and vowed to serve Him with all of his heart if the plane landed safely … and it did. It was this story and others that she listened to over and over again because that's what pastors' wives did.

Sometimes, however, Rosalee chimed in with a sarcastic witty comment when Melvin spoke, and the entire church grinned and laughed because she was quite funny! In fact, Rosalee had a great sense humor and pulled out sayings that no one had ever heard before.

One particular conversation between Melvin and Rosalee went something like this. Melvin commented, "I don't even want to vote, but I know I have to."

Rosalee quickly replied, "You don't have to do anything but pay taxes and die."

Another time, her hilarious humor shined forth in a talk with her son. Rosalee asked, "What is that bread I like at the sandwich place?"

Her son replied, "Ciabatta."

Rosalee thought for a second and commented, "Hmmm … okay, just don't do it in my backyard!"

Somehow Rosalee got pleasure out of being a little bit naughty, but not quite all the way. She even wore a t-shirt that said, "Well behaved women don't make history." So she misbehaved, just a teensy bit, within the confines of her faith and role as a pastor's wife. It was her way of releasing the tension between the stifled expectations of the do's and don'ts of church life and the freedom of living life large as a woman of passion and funniness. She adored her family and kids and grandkids, and enjoyed making them laugh out loud.

However, there just wasn't enough of the laughing or the joy in Rosalee's life. Her darkness, her drowning sensation, and her lack of ability to swim like a fish was now becoming simply treading in water. She wasn't really moving forward, but she'd found a way to wiggle herself just enough to stay afloat with her head held high. She was good at what she did in her business, she was surrounded by a growing family that loved her and her idiosyncrasies, and she was finding her own contentment in being herself. It was a hard thing to do when the church bench was beneath you, hard and immovable.

CHAPTER 29

The Lifesaver

Rosalee, like all moms, enjoyed seeing her children thrive. She celebrated each birth of a new child, showed up with gifts in hand for new homes being built, exploded with kind words on jobs well done, and believed the sun rose and set with each child's accomplishments and awards. So when her son lost his firstborn child, the grief she saw on his face and that of the mother of their child was too much to bear.

This just couldn't be happening, could it?

When her youngest daughter and her husband built their dream home on a couple of acres outside of town, Rosalee showed up to help set up house. She and her daughter even accidentally tore up a child's blanket to use for dusting rags (the son of one of the workers had left it on the counter), and realized they'd wounded this child forever! Rosalee helped line the shelves, and Melvin came out to plant trees. And then her daughter and son-in-law ended up losing the house a few years later, due to unforeseen circumstances and a poor economy. Her heart ached for their loss.

Rosalee could not fix what was wrong. If she could have brought back her dying grandchild, she would have. If she could have saved the lost house for her daughter, she would have. If money could have brought back the baby or kept the house, Rosalee would have spent all she had. But money couldn't solve these problems.

Later on, her son and his wife parted ways, as did her eldest granddaughter and her husband. Family, which was supposed to be forever, was now broken. And hearts were wounded. Healing was needed.

All of the years of sermons on giving and receiving flashed through Rosalee's mind. Asking and receiving, believing and knowing: the formulas that had worked were now broken.

Or were they?

She'd heard it all, about how if tithes are paid to the church, finances at home will be plenty. If one was faithful, blessings would be theirs. Love was the key, the greatest even above faith and hope. She'd heard it all a hundred times over.

And yet sadness had visited her children and her grandchildren, and heartbreak had left its mark.

Rosalee remembered how her dad had loved, even when he was teased and abused by his parishioners. She recalled how her mom had loved even when Rosalee almost killed her by flipping the car. Melvin too was still there, grieving with the children, right beside her, and that brought comfort.

"God, I can't fix my kids' broken hearts," she cried out as she prayed and prayed for comfort and understanding, hoping to be heard.

Rosalee continued to call her children and ask how they were doing. And then she stayed awake at night, praying for them to see God's goodness manifest in their lives.

Either the God who called her husband to be a preacher against her wishes was true … or He was not.

Either Jesus who saved people from hell was real, near and able to heal ... or He was not.

At the same time, her children were wrestling with the same questions. And Rosalee was right there with them in the ring as they were getting socked, knocked down, and left for the count to begin.

As her son was drowning in sorrow, Rosalee began throwing in lifesavers of hope through her faith in her heavenly Father. This lifesaver of hope had been thrown to her back when her own dad had tried to take his life, all because of his questions and wrestling with God. That lifesaver came seemingly out of nowhere and lifted her up above the rising waters. And then she knew it was from above. And here it was again, only this time she needed to toss a lifesaver to her family. And she did.

CHAPTER 30

Sayings and Strokes

Rosalee was often found humming tunes from her teen years, and she churned out more old sayings that made everyone laugh.

When her daughter called to ask, "What are you doing, Mom?" Rosalee often replied as she did as a young girl, "Just juning around."

For years, the kids thought that was a made-up phrase until one decided to Google it and found it was indeed a saying originating in Arkansas, where Rosalee had lived as a child! It just meant she was messing around, not doing much. She'd been using that phrase since she was a little girl, back when her mom asked her the same question about what she was doing. It was an endearing phrase that would end up stitched on a pillow, sitting on a sofa, in the youngest daughter's home.

These sayings and tunes were Rosalee's way of lighting up the room and entering into conversation when family gathered. When she was in a good mood (not pondering her childhood, preacher's wife woes, or her children's losses), she was quite silly. Granny ... and Mom ... were one and the same: one delightful lady.

There were other days when Rosalee dug in her heels and work was all there was, all that needed to be done, and there was no time for play at all. Sun up till sun down, she carried on in her office with vigor and tenacity to make sure all of the employees were on task, without a mistake to be made. She carried on like this for years as her family continued to grow, and she worked more so that she could give more.

This very interesting woman was either completely silly and funny or serious and solemn. She watched her children make their own way through the waters of life; they didn't know how to swim very well, either. Storms rose and subsided, but the family all stayed afloat together through laughter, faith, and family time together around the table.

Even though Rosalee still had never stepped foot in the water or taught a single child to swim, her family was making strokes that were gaining momentum and strength in this stormy sea called life.

CHAPTER 31

Pies and Cakes

One particular Christmas, Rosalee took the entire family of children, grandchildren, and great grandkids to San Diego, California, for an amazing holiday affair. This was years later, after decades of piled-up gifts around the tree at her home. It was when she was older, tired easily, and money was more plentiful than energy to cook, clean, and host. It was after multiple holidays of baked pecan pies and German chocolate cake. It was time to take this large family away for relaxation and fun.

Speaking of those pecan pies that had shown up year after year, this was one connection Melvin and Rosalee had that held them together like the syrup held the pecans into place. He picked out pecans he had gathered from his gigantic pecan tree in the front yard and other trees around town, and she made pies. This tradition started way back when they both sold pecans for extra income. Their dream of a big pecan tree in the front yard and pecan pies baking in the oven had come true.

Anyone that tasted Rosalee's pies was hooked—line and sinker—and wanted more. Even though she had stopped fishing with Melvin long ago (because of that no-pant rule), she was reeling in hungry fish by the droves to enjoy her baked creation. And by the way, she was now wearing pants while she stirred and baked!

What progress!

September through December, one could find Melvin in the garage with stains on his fingers from the pecan shells he had opened. Rosalee was in the kitchen with sticky fingers from the Karo syrup she'd stirred into her batter. They had found a way to be together over their love of giving and sharing, and it fulfilled one of those longings in both of their hearts for love.

One cannot forget the German chocolate cake, either. The icing was full of those same pecans, with whole pieces and broken pieces mixed into the caramel topping that drizzled over the top, across each layer, and onto the plate at the base. In fact, those pecans and that syrup were just like her family: some whole and some broken, but all sweet and stuck together! It was a cake to be enjoyed by all, year after year.

Rosalee and Melvin's relationship also had been full of broken pieces, unfulfilled dreams, lonely days and disappointed hopes, much like those cracked pecans that had been broken apart. However, broken pecans are the best part of the icing on a cake. Everyone who saw and met this duo left knowing they had tasted something uniquely stacked in flavor and goodness.

Yes, Christmas in San Diego, in a large condo with the ocean in view, was grand. But so was Christmas at home with pie and cake in hand.

CHAPTER 32

The Idiot Walk

Rosalee had a unique form of exercise in her later years. It was called her "idiot walk." She had never been an outdoorsy woman or athletic in any sense of the word, so walking on trails or in parks wasn't really her thing. She suffered from allergies. Due to that fact, exercising outdoors was not good for her health.

Rosalee also had a saying for good health, and it seemed to work well for her. It was, "All things in moderation."

Oh, she ate fruits and vegetables often, but there were many afternoons she'd be seen standing behind the counter in the kitchen enjoying a Snickers bar. She was all for staying healthy, but she wasn't going to be a stickler about restrictions and/or jogging the trails. She had had enough restrictions in so many other areas of her life.

Back to the idiot walk …

Rosalee started at one end of the house and walked around each room at a quick pace, round and round, through the halls and back, wearing her walking shoes! It didn't matter that she wasn't outdoors, on a trail, at the beginning of track … she was dressed for the activity. She created her own track, so to speak: her own tailored exercise routine just for idiots like her, she teased. She often wore velour pantsuits with a cute tee underneath the jacket, and donned her black tennis shoes, tied snuggly so that she could walk at a fast pace.

"I'm going on my idiot walk," she announced as she got up and started moving.

If anyone was in earshot, he or she smiled, and Rosalee did too. However, Rosalee was anything but an idiot. She might not know one thing about how far or fast she needed to walk, how to perform a perfect breast stroke in swimming, or even how to dance one step in a waltz, but she knew healthy living meant moving often—and cleaning off that makeup nightly, which Rosalee did.

"Marcy, don't ever go to sleep with your makeup on," she often instructed her daughter when she was a teen. And Marcy never did.

One more piece of funny trivia about this incredible lady is that she cleaned her floors with a cloth that she moved around with her foot! Down on the floor she'd throw a rag, and then she'd place her foot on top and swish back and forth. This too was part of her exercise routine while she cleaned. A two-for-one!

All of this, and more, kept her moving and thriving and surviving … and living.

CHAPTER 33

No Holes

Rosalee had quite the collection of jewelry. One year, she was given one of those freestanding jewelry armoires, and it was soon full. She had an array of smaller jewelry boxes atop one of her dressers, and it too was lined with pretties. She loved to find that perfect necklace or pair of earrings to match her outfits, as she had already trained her fashion eye from all those years of watching girls on the square with her best friend, Lovey.

Clip-on earrings were her favorite.

Rosalee was asked many times, "Why don't you get your ears pierced?" especially by her kids who had a hard time finding clip-ons each birthday and Christmas.

Rosalee's answer was the same each time she was asked, "If God had wanted another hole in my ears, He would have put it there."

And then she'd smile that million-dollar smile, and her kids would keep shopping and finding those elusive clip-ons in gold and silver and all kinds of colors.

When she wore her jewelry, her outfits shined. If Rosalee had become a famous fashion designer, there's no doubt she would have included a jewelry line as well! She just had that eye that could spot the perfect piece to enhance that perfect outfit for that perfect look. Each time she stepped out for church or fun, or dinner, she had on a little something different just like she did with that skewed collar on that awesome dress she'd sewn so many years earlier.

Holes in the ears? No way.

But bracelets on the wrists, necklaces round the neck, and clips on her lobes? Yes!

She loved them all.

CHAPTER 34

November 2

With magazine sales booming, the office chairs full, life was good.

Another wedding anniversary was nearing, and Rosalee had long since quit wishing for a romantic night out with Melvin. He just wasn't that kind of husband. Anniversaries Melvin loved to celebrate were the church kind: another year as pastor. There were all kinds of fanfare for that anniversary, but not so much for another year of marriage. She did receive flowers sometimes, but not a date night out like she saw her children enjoy with their spouses.

Rosalee often resented those other anniversaries of the church kind because they made her feel less important than a building or a position or a group of people.

But here it was, November 2, and she wanted to celebrate. Her daughter and her family were on their way to a soccer game and stopped by to pick up Melvin and Rosalee to join them for the fun. However, it was raining. And it was raining hard. Rosalee and Melvin opted out of the ride and decided to sit this one out at home and wait to hear later how their grandson, the defense player, would fare at the game.

It was a sad day, though, when they received a call later in the day after the game was over and learned that one of the players had been killed in an auto accident. Rosalee's daughter and family witnessed the event. Not only was the little boy lost, but so were his mother and grandmother, on the slick roads from the rain.

Rosalee's tears from earlier in the day, wishing that this anniversary might be different, had subsided. And she now shed tears in sorrow and horror for the loss of her grandson's best buddy.

She turned to her husband and gave thanks as they prayed together all night for comfort and rest for their family, comfort that could only come from above. She'd learned that taking his hand, then bowing their heads, was one connection that held power to move heaven ... and power to keep them together.

CHAPTER 35

Vacation

Every summer, Melvin and Rosalee boarded a plane to go see the other daughter who lived in California: the daughter who married and moved away the day after the wedding. Too far away.

At first, Melvin and Rosalee resisted and detested this young man who dared to interrupt the family unit by moving one member two thousand miles across the country. But over time, and after the birth of their very first grandchild, it was on a plane they were found, again escaping the Texas heat to step out into the sunny cool breezes of Northern California.

A vacation with Granny and Papa was like none other. When they showed up or went anywhere, they always invited the entire family to come, all expenses paid. Rosalee enjoyed paying for dinners, sightseeing excursions, shopping sprees, and more. Even when she stayed behind to rest, she tucked cash into each girl's hand and said, "It's not much. But go find you something pretty."

When the girls returned with their bags in hand, Rosalee was the first one to ask to see, and the first one to exclaim, "That is so cute."

It was quite the learning lesson to observe this woman give. Her hands may have never glided through the ocean waves to be swept and carried away, but she sure knew how to open her hands to freely give to others. She may not have known how to swim, but she taught others how to enjoy the complete ocean unafraid, and offered them a hand up and a breath of fresh air with her giving spirit.

That's exactly what it felt like to receive that wad of cash from Granny, or Mom, because each kid at one time or another needed a little extra something to buy a fun desire of their heart.

That hand-up that she offered so often kept the entire family clothed in their finest, housed with pretty furnishings, and having fun all over the place, even when life hit with sorrow, trouble, or unexpected downfalls.

CHAPTER 36

Hearing

Later in life, Rosalee grew hard of hearing, as many do when they age. Her dad had been the same. Now as Rosalee aged, she was unable to hear well too. It was a slow process, that loss of hearing, but there it was nonetheless: an unwelcome guest for sure. Even with hearing aids, when she was out at a restaurant with the family, the noises around her would render those aids useless, and Rosalee was unable to really enter into conversations around the table.

Of course, Rosalee smiled and nodded and even replied at times, but often it was a reply to what she *thought* she heard, not what was said.

One time, back when her kids were younger, Rosalee's dad was playing dominoes with them. That was one game Charles Blevins loved to play! This particular game was a serious one (weren't they all?), and he was playing with Rosalee's son and youngest daughter. Everyone was quiet as they awaited Charles' next play, and one of the grandchildren farted. Giggles ensued quietly, as they didn't think Papa Blevins had heard, but he did.

He looked up with a grin and commented, "Someone had a blow out," as the entire table burst into laughter.

Lesson learned?

Apparently, some sounds come through loud and clear (or was it the smell?), even to those who are hard of hearing.

Rosalee's hearing wasn't so good toward the end, and when she entered the hospital for that final stay, it was her daughter's privilege and honor to be asked to change her mom's hearing aids daily, which included replacing the battery and inserting the aids just right into the ear canal. It wasn't an easy or particularly pleasurable job because her daughter grew queasy quite easily, but it was something that needed to be done for Mom. Each time that little aid slipped into place, Rosalee smiled and nodded, "Good."

And even with the best of hearing aids she could find, Rosalee's hearing still suffered. Nurses and doctors entered the room and asked questions (it seemed they never could remember to speak up!) and shared information about Rosalee's condition. However, Rosalee had to look to her daughter for clarity as those trained professionals left the room.

It was important for Rosalee to be heard those last few weeks of her life because she was hurting in a bad way. But it was equally important for Rosalee to hear, so the family had learned to speak up and speak clearly so that she could hear and understand. It was the least everyone could do to offer a hand back to her as she began sinking into a sea of surgery and decline.

Each member of the family had learned how to swim in this sea of life from a great woman and also knew how to enjoy every moment thanks to a lady who had never stepped foot into an actual pool of water of any size.

Hand over hand, cupping and pulling, gliding and giving, sharing all that you have was what they had learned.

There was always room in the ocean of life for laughter, hilarity, and fun.

CHAPTER 37

Stories

Rosalee's brother often told the story of how his parents disciplined him as a child, and Rosalee shared that same very disturbingly odd story with her children, as mentioned earlier in this book. When Charlie was bad, Charles and Lina required him to sit on the front porch in girls' clothes. This shamed Charlie for misbehaving, or at least that was the intent. Of course, just as Rosalee had been when she'd first heard the story, her children were appalled at this treatment and considered it to be abuse for sure.

Another story told from childhood was one of Rosalee's pigtails. She wore her hair in long braids when she was in grade school, and sometimes the boy behind her dipped one of her pigtails into the ink pot on the desk. One day, Rosalee had had quite enough of this boy's shenanigans, and with a big bop on the head, she clobbered the youngster with her umbrella. The boy never touched Rosalee again and left her pigtails swinging from her head instead of swimming in ink.

Childhood was a daily routine of following strict rules in the Blevins' household, under the thumb of Rosalee's preacher dad and her mom. Charles did not allow Rosalee to cut her long hair or wear red lipstick as a young girl, two of Rosalee's desires. She dreamed of the day she could wear her hair in that new bob style that was so popular among the other girls and swipe her lips with that ruby-red stain. So until that day came when she had the choice to do these two things (age thirteen), Rosalee found a way to wear her hair in a bob without having scissors touch her hair! She gathered the ends together, took a long ribbon, and tied it at the base of her hair. She then tucked that part of her hair under, pulling the ribbon up around the top of her head, and tied it in a bow. The hair was turned under, sat right above her shoulders, and gave the appearance of a bob! Once again, Rosalee's creativity shined through. However, she never quite figured out how to stain her lips until she actually had that small tube of creamy redness in her hands …

When that day arrived, she stepped into Woolworths, found a tube of Red Ransom, and bought it. She smeared it on just to the edge of her smile and walked out with a new confidence to face the world. Rosalee's red lips were now her favorite accessory, even before she wore that skewed collar a few years later.

CHAPTER 38

Tummy Aches

As Rosalee grew older, it was obvious at times that her sadness was still a veil over her face, but there were more instances of her happiness that shone through. Her kids knew that she suffered from loneliness, that she and Melvin weren't the romantic couple she had hoped they would be, and that pastor's wife (which she had now been for almost sixty years) still wasn't the life she had wanted. However, Rosalee had settled into the knowing, the rest, the peace that comes from swimming through life with Him as a lifesaver and teacher of how to kick one's feet and move one's arms in order to stay afloat and enjoy the water.

She often had tummy aches but alieved the pain with various pills for that sort of thing. Her legs grew a bit wobblier, and she sometimes experienced vertigo. So she succumbed to walking with a cane. She didn't mind, though, because it offered her stability.

Sometimes, when shopping with her youngest daughter, she apologized by stating, "I'm sorry I'm being so slow."

But her daughter never minded it one bit because shopping with Mom was the best. She absolutely delighted in every new thing on the shelf, the colors of a new season, and the opportunity to buy lunch or a new outfit for whomever was with her on the excursion.

A couple of instances of tummy pain found Rosalee in the ER with family by her bedside, but she was sent home with meds for a urinary infection or the pain subsided, and back to normal life they all went.

CHAPTER 39

Mom's Day

Mother's Day 2017 was another celebration where the family got together for dinner at a Mexican restaurant, one of Rosalee's favorite kinds of food. She loved to go out to eat and did so almost every night of the week with her son and her husband as she grew older. The family gathered, and she opened her gifts, one of which included a cute white t-shirt and a lovely cover-up given to her by her daughter. Rosalee had long since stopped sewing because her magazine business required all of her time, so her daughter enjoyed treating Mom with a new outfit on days to celebrate. There was always another outfit waiting in the mail, as well, from the daughter in California. Both daughters always tried to find Mom something a bit different because they knew she loved anything out of the ordinary.

That afternoon, Rosalee's daughter and son-in-law took Melvin and Rosalee to a park for a walk, to sit on a bench and enjoy the birds and a lake in view. They soon heard the sound of a peddler with frozen treats approaching. He was pushing his cart down the sidewalk, and it was definitely a welcome sight. Rosalee and Melvin always had an "extra stomach" for sweets, so her daughter was so happy to buy Rosalee a mango-flavored iced treat. As Rosalee and Melvin walked toward the bench to sit down and enjoy their treats, their daughter snapped a photo. It was obvious in the faces of these two people—one already in his 90s and Rosalee approaching that same decade soon—that they loved each other, loved life, loved Him, and loved time with their children.

The years of wondering why, bickering over decisions and mandates, showing up faithfully to serve when those receiving were ungrateful and unknowing, had taken a toll on their bodies and spirits. *But* they had both emerged beautifully whole and sweetly smitten by their faith in the One who holds us all together in the storm, above the waves, and through the darkness. Their daughter looked on with wonder, as she too had often grown weary with her parents' issues. But she loved them nonetheless. She snapped a photo of their loveliness, and one of her and her mom as well, since they were both wearing orange that day!

The twinkle in her mom's eyes was priceless!

The four of them, Rosalee and Melvin, Marcy and her husband Jon, sat on one bench together, swinging their feet and eating their treats. In view was a lovely pond with birds landing and flying, over and over again. There were other families present with their children, and their mothers, enjoying the beautiful weather in the month of May. It was a picture-perfect scene.

CHAPTER 40

Surgery and Nail Polish

That very week found the family back at the ER with Rosalee, as once again her stomach was hurting badly. This time when tests were done, it was revealed that there was a gall stone in a tube that needed to be removed. The surgery was performed the next day, and all was supposed to be well until the family was informed that a small perforation had occurred in the tube when the removal of the stone was made. No worries, however, as this hole would heal over time … but the surgeon also needed to remove her entire gall bladder. Back into surgery this eighty-nine-year-young woman went. She emerged completely whole and ready to recover and get back home.

That first night in the hospital, Rosalee had arrived with lipstick on and nails painted in a beautiful hue of orange, one that matched the blouse she had worn on Mother's Day. Many of the nurses noted how pretty Rosalee's nails were, and Rosalee asked her daughter, "Would you get several bottles (which meant fifty) of this nail polish and set them out on the table, one for each nurse to take?"

Of course, Marcy agreed to find the polish and set out each one and give them all away. The nurses were delighted!

No one had ever made that request, and no one had ever given them all such a selfless gift!

By the end of the week, it was evident that the hole in Rosalee's tube was not healing, and she was extremely ill. The surgeon sat down with the family and explained the rerouting procedure he could do with her stomach, a very serious surgery, but hopefully with a great outcome. There was no choice but to say yes, and Rosalee went in for a third surgery.

This time the recovery process started out in the ICU with a tube down her throat, and a few days of the family sitting near.

One day, Marcy even heard her mom cry out, "Mother," as she was waking up.

Did she see her mom? Marcy wondered.

Back on the floor, in a regular room, the family gathered day after day as Rosalee slowly tried to recover. Physical therapy came, but very little movement was made. Rosalee's body was weak and tired. She was unable to eat yet, so little cups of crushed ice were offered to her, upon request. Her family sat with her and did foot exercises with her as she tried to keep her muscles flexible and strong. However, Rosalee's comfort was never found as she constantly asked nurses and techs to rearrange her bed, scoot her up, and adjust her pillows. Her youngest grandson even fitted the chair in the room with pillows and sheets so that it was perfectly comfortable for Granny. It was a very hard ten days or so as the family sat and hoped and waited for healing to take place.

Finally, that day came when the doctor allowed Rosalee to sip something other than melted ice and taste a bit of food.

That was one glorious day, especially for Melvin. And the doctor said Rosalee was ready to be moved to a rehab facility to start therapy to gain her strength again to move about and return home.

CHAPTER 41

The Last Biscuit

The ambulance came, and Marcy rode next to the driver while Rosalee was on a stretcher in the back with the attendants. The room was being prepared for her at the facility on a Friday afternoon. Rosalee's granddaughter came to hang words of encouragement on a bulletin board. Other grandchildren came to visit, bringing gifts and ideas to help her maintain hope. Her son's grandkids made special cards, applying their artwork and sentiments, and these too were hung in perfect order. Being that it was Friday, the family was told not much would happen over the weekend, but therapy would indeed start on Monday.

Saturday morning came, and Rosalee was brought her breakfast: a real one with a biscuit on the plate! Melvin pulled up a chair to the hospital rolling tray and they ate, together.

Rosalee commented, "Marcy, this is so good," and Melvin smiled as he too ate a bite. And then another bite …

Eating was one of their intense pleasures that they enjoyed doing together, and neither one knew this would be their last meal together this side of that place above.

Rosalee's stomach began to hurt, and back to bed she

went. By Monday morning, it just seemed something wasn't quite right. Rosalee's granddaughter-in-law arrived with a cute headband for Rosalee to wear, as her hair had not been fixed since her arrival in the hospital three weeks prior. It was June 12, and Rosalee was in a chair, trying to muster up strength for the day.

Rosalee's daughter and son took turns during that stay at the hospital and rehab facility, the daughter taking the early morning to afternoon shift, with the son taking the afternoon to late night shift. Melvin showed up every day, faithfully sitting by her side, even though Rosalee had checked out of normal life and was focused on her pain. The daughter and son-in-law from California visited as well, helping out with Mom and Dad.

That Monday afternoon, Rosalee grabbed her stomach and began to convey to the nurse that something wasn't right. A few hours later, after some tests, she was in an ambulance again, this time with her son, on the way back to the ER at the hospital. As the ambulance attendants were wheeling Rosalee to the emergency vehicle, she held out her hand toward her son as fear gripped her heart—much like the fear she'd had when she tried to think about swimming in a deep pool of water where things were unknown and unseen.

The family was called, and they gathered at the hospital as they were told very shortly after arrival that she was not making it … about to die … and they could come in and say their goodbyes. Hope waned, and she passed, with each family member around her bedside watching her take her last breaths.

Was she afraid?

Was she in pain?

Was she aware they were near?

And then it was announced. She was gone.

Rosalee passed from this life to that next one, the one she sang about, to the place where Jesus was with His hand stretched out to hold hers—the place where all of her pain and suffering would be gone ... forever.

Stunned.

Saddened.

Confused.

Wondering.

The family went through the motions of planning a funeral, celebrating a life, and comforting a dad/grandfather. An autopsy was paid for, and they waited.

Weeks later, it was learned that the stomach tube in Rosalee's abdomen had shifted and cut a hole in her stomach, which caused her death.

There was anger. There was frustration. There was sadness all over again. Poor Mom suffered so intensely, even though, relatively speaking, it was a short stay in the hospital. It was a hard one to watch, to experience with her, and to be there when she left, but they were all thankful she was no longer in pain.

CHAPTER 42

Come In!

Another few weeks passed, and Rosalee's youngest daughter was in church one Sunday morning, not because she had to be there, but because she loved to worship there. Thankfully, she hadn't lived under that dutiful attendance rule, but rather realized the privilege of community with others. She asked under her breath, "What are you doing, Mom? Where are you?"

In that moment, she *saw* her mom in a pool of water, splashing and playing like a kid, looking right at her and saying, "Come in. This is so fun!"

What a moment that was because the daughter realized that the first thing upon her mom's arrival into heaven was that she was given the erasure of the fear of swimming, that fear that had been with her the entire time she was on the earth. The pleasure she was forbidden to experience because of religious trappings was now an experience she was given to enjoy without fear and without guilt. There was only unchained joy.

So it really was true ... this new life with Him after the one she'd struggled with since a child under a tent, listening to the calls to repent! All the prayers she'd prayed, all the songs she had sang, yet nothing compared to the look on His face when He offered His hand to come in and step out of the sinking sand into the water to play. To play! Not to work!

Who knew that never learning to swim as a little girl would be the first gift of eternity, an invitation to swim freely? This dying woman was made alive again with the One she loved so dearly, more than life itself.

It was the first thing her heavenly Father attended to upon arrival to the other side: that removal of all fear of the unknown.

"Come in!" the youngest daughter heard again as tears flowed down her face. She too was encouraged once again by her mom, though she was gone and not present beside her. Those words were an invitation, a declaration, an exclamation of the joy that was hers, and she wanted her daughter to know all was well and good.

CHAPTER 43

Unafraid

As the sun rises and sets each day, each member of the family remembers Mom, Rosalee, Granny, in different outfits, on different occasions, and in different ways. Some of the grandkids recall sitting down with Granny as she emptied her purse of loose change, making sure each kid got a handful of coins to spend or save. Other grandkids sit on their furniture and give thanks for this generous woman who shared all that she had with those that she loved. One daughter recalls those shopping excursions and the other daughter those long-awaited visits as her mom stepped off the plane. The son misses his nightly dinners with Mom as she so enjoyed a good meal. And Melvin hums longingly those lyrics of the song about the hand he misses now and longs to hold, the hand that's holding His up above. And many friends and coworkers miss Rosalee's smile and funniness and charm and loveliness as she stepped into a room and brought light with her wherever she went.

But most of all, each of them remembers those hands that swam lovingly through life as they opened to receive and then stayed open to give, even though this lady never learned a single breaststroke in the water.

They all recall the simple yet powerful prayer she prayed over each meal, "Father, we're grateful."

And there she is now, splashing and calling and swimming quite well,

"Won't you come in? Swimming with Him is all the rage when you're unafraid …"

Printed in the United States
By Bookmasters